TIMOTHY FL[...]

BABY HAYNES

A TRUE STORY ABOUT ADOPTION AND UNCONDITIONAL LOVE

★★★★★★★★

★★★★

I came into this great, big world like any other baby racehorse. I was born from my mommy's tummy into a warm bed of straw.

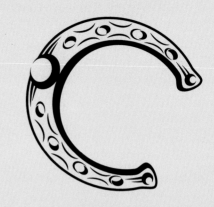

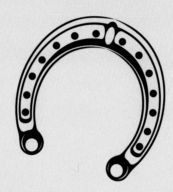

I quickly grew strength in my wobbly legs.

AFTER
    ONE,
        TWO
            THREE TRIES, I stood up
and I was running around my stall and playing!

My mommy's racing name was

IN VITRO.

She was a winning racehorse from the racetrack and very fast.

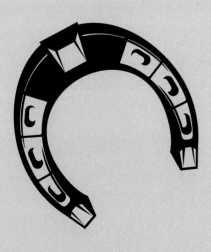

IN VITRO
MY BEAUTIFUL MOMMY

Her daddy, my grandpa, was the famous Washington Champion racehorse, *Demon Warlock.* I have big plans to someday follow in the hoof-steps of my very successful family.

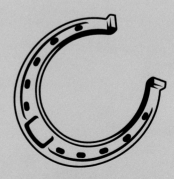

DEMON WARLOCK,
MY HANDSOME GRANDPA

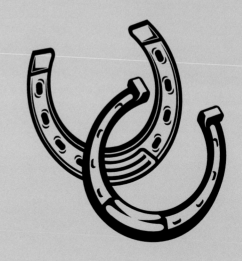

MY BEAUTIFUL DADDY, HAYNESFIELD

My daddy, Haynesfield, is a great-grandson of the greatest racehorse of all-time, *Secretariat!!*

So, do you know what that means? ★★★★

I am related to **"BIG RED,"** too! My daddy, Haynesfield, also defeated Blame, the only horse to ever beat the mighty Zenyatta! I have some famous relatives in my family tree, including Northern Dancer, the 1964 Kentucky Derby winner and very famous sire.

My daddy and I share the same exact star on our forehead.
I hope I can run like him. He won a race at

 BELMONT PARK,
THE JOCKEY CLUB GOLD CUP,

by four lengths. This is a very important and prestigious race.

Many people believe my great-great-grandpa, **Secretariat** was the best racehorse ever, and I sure do agree. There are **three** famous races that make up the **Triple Crown:**

THE KENTUCKY DERBY, THE PREAKNESS *and*  THE BELMONT STAKES

SECRETARIAT *HAS THE FASTEST* *TIME IN ALL THREE!*

My daddy's great-great-grandpa!
CHAMPION SECRETARIAT

I spend my days frolicking in the fields with other babies. We all hope to one day be champion racehorses. My friends and I love to feel the warm sun on our backs and wind in our manes. We love to spend the days kicking up our heels!

One night when I was still very young, my mommy got a very bad tummy ache. She was very sick, and I was very worried and scared.

Many horse doctors, called veterinarians, came to see her to try to make her feel better. But, no matter how hard they tried, they couldn't heal my mommy.

She kissed me goodbye and went to heaven.

 MY MOMMY,
IN VITRO

The next morning, I was very thirsty for milk. I could hear people talking about how to help me. I was led into a strange new room that started to move! I was in a horse trailer and I was scared but I was excited, too! I had never been in something like this and I was all alone. I decided to lay down and rest for a while. After five long hours, the trailer came to a stop.

YOU CAN'T SEE ME, BUT I AM IN THE TRAILER! MY FRIEND, ROSE, DID A GREAT JOB GETTING ME TO MY NEW HOME.

I didn't know what to expect, but I was very hungry and thirsty for more milk. Some very nice people took me into a big, beautiful barn. That's where I met the strangest looking horse that I had ever seen. My mommy and my friends were all a solid color. But this horse, also a mommy horse, had big patches of white and brown.

This strange-looking mommy horse started to whinny and nicker at me. All the nice people smiled. They wanted us to get close to each other, and it was working. We were forming a special bond!

WHAT A GREAT TEAM!

I could tell this mommy horse was sad, too. Her baby had gone to heaven just like my mommy did. She wanted a baby horse to call her own and I wanted a mommy. We could help each other. And, I was still hungry. I could smell her sweet mommy milk. I decided to take a drink. It tasted so good. I was so hungry that I couldn't stop! She was so nice to share with me. She let me have all I wanted and nuzzled me while I drank.

MOMMY HORSE, ☞
ALLURE *and*
BABY HAYNES

I was beginning to believe I had found my new home. Now I spend days frolicking in the field with my wonderful new mommy! She always keeps me by her side, and she protects me. She loves me and I love her back.

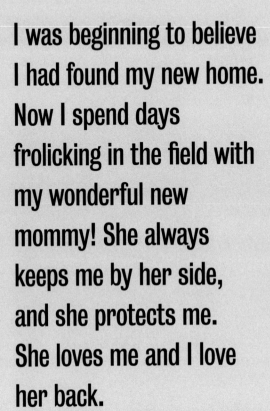

This is my friend, Kenny. He takes care of the farm I call my new home. He feeds us in the morning and in the evening. He also makes sure our feet are trimmed and teaches us how to lead like big horses.

This is the great shipper, Rose, who made sure I arrived safely to my new friends and family. She is very sweet.

This is the nice doctor who takes very good care of the horses at my new home. His name is Dr. Golden.

Not long after I got my new mommy, the local news team came out and did a great story on us to share with the world, so I am kind of a celebrity at the farm with my friends.

My new mommy trains me on how to run so I can one-day be a champion racehorse.

My new mommy also teaches me that we don't have to look alike to be family.

SHE HAS SPOTS AND I HAVE RED HAIR!

My new mommy shows me how to be a good and loving horse, by being a proud and loving mommy.

7

My big brother, *Verynsky*, is already a winning racehorse. He lives with us at the farm and I learn a lot from him, too.

 MY BIG BROTHER, **VERYNSKY,** IS A VERY FAST RACEHORSE!

★ ★ ★ ★

I still love my first mommy and I will always remember her. I also love my new home. I love sharing it with my new mommy, my big brother and all my friends. We love each other and protect each other.

WE ARE A FAMILY.

After spending a very snowy winter playing with my friends and family, I am now a yearling, which means I am one year old and a big boy like my pasture buddies. After my second birthday, I get to be a racehorse and I can't wait!

 The snow has melted, and summer has arrived and so has my big, strong body!! I am now a yearling and growing fast. I could be joining my brother at the racetrack in less than one year. I can't wait to show them how fast I am!!

MY HOME, WHERE I WILL LEARN TO *be a* CHAMPION!!

THE END
AND BEGINNING
OF A GREAT JOURNEY!